World War I

Researching American History

introduced and edited by
Pat Perrin

U.S. Coast Artillery, firing the 340mm gun. (National Archives)

Discovery Enterprises, Ltd.
Carlisle, Massachusetts

First Edition © Discovery Enterprises, Ltd., Carlisle, MA 2001

ISBN: 1-57960-075-1

Library of Congress Catalog Card Number 2001093163

10   9   8   7   6   5   4   3   2   1

Printed in the United States of America

Subject Reference Guide:

Title: *World War I*
Series*: Researching American History*
introduced and edited by Pat Perrin

World War I

Credits:

Cover photo: "Removing the wounded."

Most photos can be found at
http://raven.cc.ukans.edu/~kansite/ww_one/photos/

Other photos are credited where they appear in the text.

Contents

About the Series

Researching American History is a series of books which introduces various topics and periods in our nation's history through the study of primary source documents.

Reading the Historical Documents

On the following pages you'll find words written by people during or soon after the time of the events. This is firsthand information about what life was like back then. Illustrations are also created to record history. These historical documents are called **primary source materials**.

At first, some things written in earlier times may seem difficult to understand. Language changes over the years, and the objects and activities described might be unfamiliar. Also, spellings were sometimes different. Below is a model which describes how we help with these challenges.

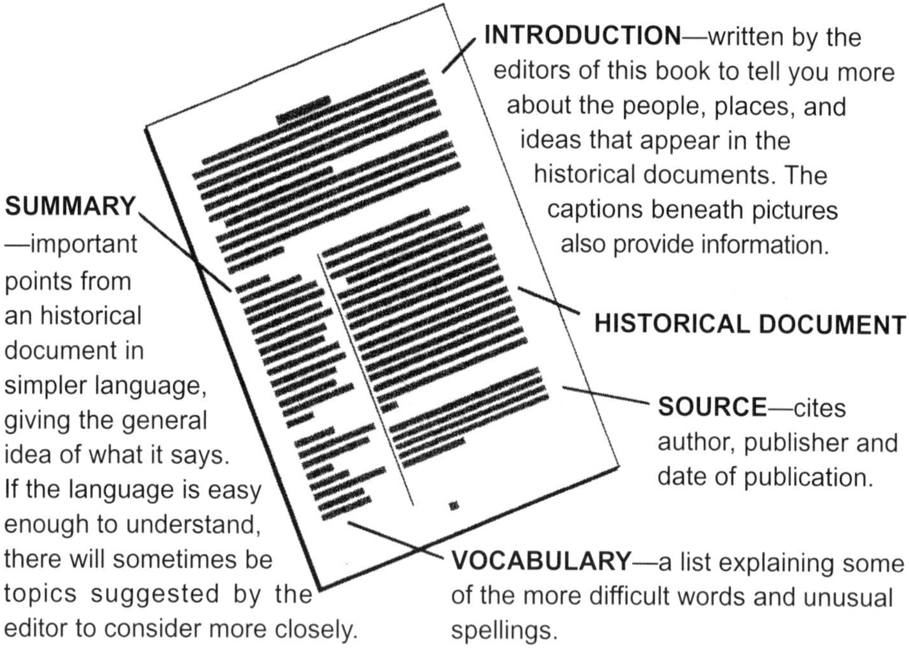

In these historical documents, you may see three periods (...) called an ellipsis. It means that the editor has left out some words or sentences. You may see some words in brackets, such as [and]. These are words the editor has added to make the meaning clearer. When you use a document in a paper you're writing, you should include any ellipses and brackets it contains, just as you see them here. Be sure to give complete information about the author, title, and publisher of anything that was written by someone other than you.

Introduction: The Great War
by Pat Perrin

The war we know as World War I was fought in Europe from 1914-1918. America officially joined the battle in 1917. It was a huge and terrible conflict that changed some of our ideas about war itself.

Instead of galloping to battle on horseback or storming across battlegrounds on foot, soldiers were crouched in ditches in the ground. Anyone charging across an open area could be cut down by new weapons before he even saw the enemy. Month after month, very little changed on the battlefront—except that more and more men died.

Still, they fought on. At that time, it was called the Great War. It involved more countries than any war had before. It killed far more people—and more brutally—than any war had before. Many people thought this would surely be the last war that nations would ever fight. It would be the war to end all wars—and to make the world safe for democracy.

World War I was long and complicated. This book doesn't try to follow battles or political actions. Instead, it tells what the war was like, in the words of people who were there. In the following pages, you'll also see what drew America into the Great War. At first, the conflict seemed very far away from our own shores.

How it Started

As the 19th century turned into the 20th, the nations of Europe had strong differences in their interests and opinions. They began to separate into two **alliances**. An alliance is an organization of nations or other groups. These alliances of European nations were made with formal written agreements, called **treaties**.

Germany, Austria-Hungary, and Italy formed the Triple Alliance. Britain, France, and Russia, who had often been fierce rivals, formed an alliance called the Triple Entente. Smaller nations joined with one side or the other. Some remained **neutral** (not supporting or favoring either side).

Both sides began building their military forces, and Europe turned into two armed camps. By 1914, Germany had the best trained soldiers and the best equipment. Britain had the greatest navy. Each side developed war plans to fight every possible combination of enemies.

In the early 20th century, there were small wars in the Balkan nations. Then it was as if the European countries were just waiting for the spark to start a major fire. That spark was struck on June 28, 1914. In the Bosnian town of Sarajevo, Archduke Franz Ferdinand—the heir to the Austrian throne—was killed by a Serb terrorist. Austria accused the Serbian government of having a hand in the assassination. International negotiations failed. On July 28, 1914, Austria-Hungary declared war on Serbia. The next day Austrian artillery fired on Belgrade, the capital of Serbia.

Russia moved against Austria, and Germany declared war against Russia. The French began to **mobilize** (prepare for war), so Germany also declared war on France. When the Germans began marching through Belgium to get to France, the British government declared war on Germany. Austria-Hungary declared war on Russia. Italy temporarily stayed neutral, but later came into the war on the side of the Allies.

*The Western Front. France, Britain, Russia, Italy, Belgium, Serbia, Montenegro Romania, Greece, Portugal, and Japan became known as the **Allies**.*

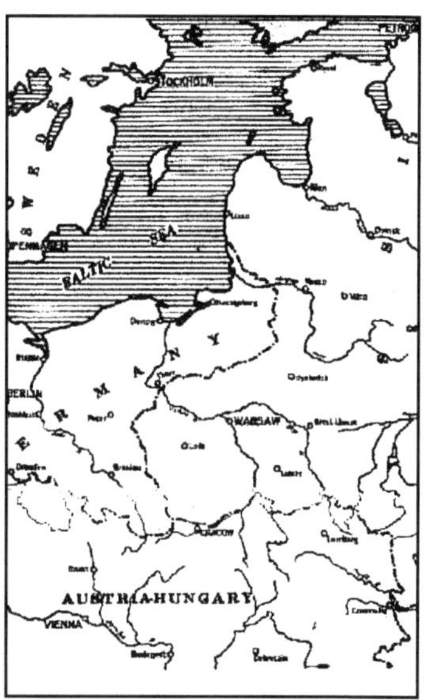

*The Eastern Front. Germany, Austria-Hungary, Turkey, and Bulgaria were called the **Central Powers**.*

The Widespread War

The Great War "spread to 28 countries on six continents. Its battles flared on land from Tsingtao, China, to the African coast, and by sea from Jutland to the Falkland Islands." (*The First World War,* by the Editors of *Life Magazine,* New York: Time Inc., 1965, p. 7.) In faraway places, legendary figures such as Lawrence of Arabia fought for local goals as well. But it was in Europe, on the Western Front, that the war had to be won. And there, Americans got into the battle.

Painting of World War I Marine, for recruiting poster. Found at http://www. scuttlebuttsmallchow.com/wwi.html

American Observers and Volunteers

From the earliest days, Americans were at the war front, even though the U.S. was not involved in the war. Some had been living in Europe when the war broke out. Some volunteered as ambulance drivers, hospital workers, and fighters. Others were sent to observe the war.

New weapons used in World War I killed and wounded soldiers at a rate never seen before. Ambulance drivers such as William Yorke Stevenson were kept constantly at work rescuing the wounded. Stevenson was a volunteer with the American Ambulance Service in France. His diaries give us some idea of what the war was like for those volunteers.

Summary:

Today the Germans shelled the road. We watched a relief driver in a tight spot.

Shells fell all around Wallace. We were all scared.

Vocabulary:

batteries = sets of guns
Boches, Germs = names
   used for Germans

An Ambulance Driver at the Front

Friday, 1 September 1916

The "Germs" shelled out the…road today, when we were on day duty…. Wallace coming to relieve us for lunch had an awfully tight squeeze making the hill while we watched him. The road there takes a big "S" turn, and the Boches were dropping [large shells] all along the lower half, trying to get the…batteries. One dropped right ahead of Wallace, and a second ten feet behind him. I don't know whether he or we were scared the worst….

Soldiers fought from trenches dug into the ground. There were hundreds of miles of trenches, connected together. They dug in and lived there. Sometimes the enemy trench line was close enough for the opposing soldiers to exchange wisecracks. Between the trench lines, the dead and sometimes the wounded were beyond reach or help.

Nobody cared to ease down to lunch, although we'd previously all agreed that we were ravenously hungry around eleven o'clock. Those appetites faded away somehow. Believe me, nobody cared for that little lofty spot, although they tell me "it's quite safe, because they're not shooting at it, but at a battery." Of course, I know that; we all do. But the same thrill gets one's spine when that nasty "ziss-bang" comes by, whether they're shooting at one or not, especially when the difference can't be more than a millimeter on the sight and is only a couple of meters at our end, seeing that we are on the edge of the ravine and our batteries are below us. If they hit us, they miss the batteries; and if they hit the batteries, they miss us. I'm (personally) quite unpatriotic when they're firing!

(continued on next page)

Summary:

We all lost our appetites. We didn't like our high spot, although they weren't shooting at us. But you still get chills when they fire, because the distance between us and the target is so small.

Vocabulary:

battery = set of guns
lofty = high up
ravenously = greedily

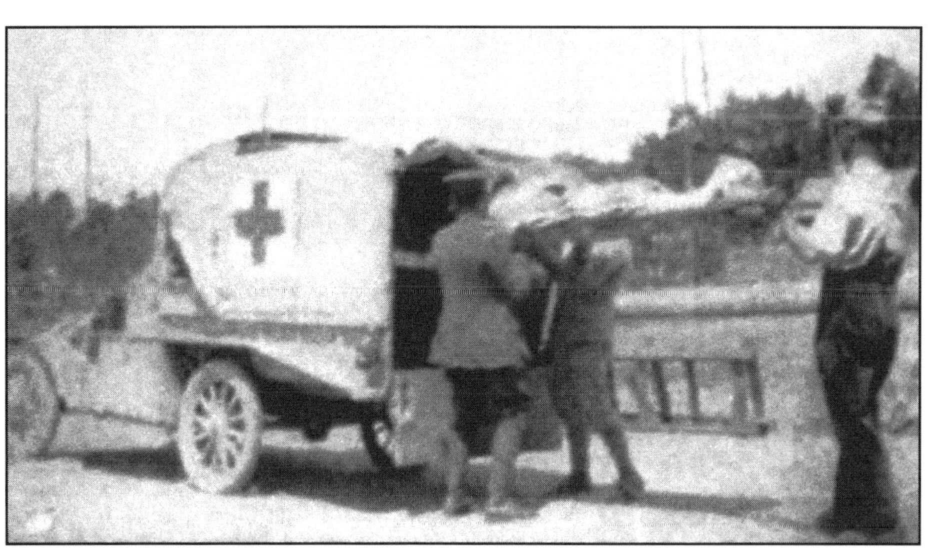

Ambulance drivers, loading the top tier of a Red Cross truck.

Summary:

After heavy fighting, the French had many prisoners.

One night a shell burst right in front of me, just as I was passing some horses. The explosion frightened the horses. I found myself surrounded by crazy animals, and nearly wrecked the ambulance. I was able to make two more trips before it broke down. Luckily I was near camp.

Vocabulary:

caissons = horse-drawn vehicles
convoy = group traveling together
ravine = deep, narrow valley or gorge
unattended = with no person in charge

Monday, 4 September 1916

For three days there has been heavy fighting…and the French got over a thousand prisoners. We have been going steadily.…

On the night of September 2, coming down with a load, a shell burst right ahead of me, just as I was passing a convoy of…ammunition caissons, the horses of which were standing, while the drivers had ducked for the roadside [ditches]. The shock and flash of the explosion, which pasted mud and stones all over the car, made the unattended horses wild. It seemed for a minute as if I was in the center of a sea of crazy animals. In avoiding them I nearly ditched the car and broke the front springs, but got away all right. Barring a wrecked side box, and a couple of rock holes in the side of the car, I was able to make two more trips before the front …gave way altogether. Luckily this occurred near our [camp].

Source: William Yorke Stevenson, *American Ambulance, At The Front In A Flivver.* Boston & NY: Houghton Mifflin Company, 1917. Found at http://raven.cc.ukans. edu/~kansite/ww_one/memoir/stevensn.htm

French attacking the German trenches.

The Red Cross is an organization with branches in most countries of the world. It provides aid to victims of war and other disasters. In World War I, the Red Cross supported volunteer ambulance drivers and operated hospitals. Many of the volunteer hospital workers were women.

Laura de Gozdawa Turczynowicz and her children after their escape from Poland.
Found at http://raven.cc.ukans.edu/~libsite/ wwi-www/Poland/Poland1.htm)

Laura de Gozdawa Turczynowicz was an American woman married to a Polish University professor. When Germany invaded Poland, she and her husband helped organize units of the Polish Red Cross and set up a hospital. A few months later, while her husband was away, the war moved in their direction. Laura, her children, and many of the wounded escaped on a Red Cross train. She later wrote a book about her experiences in Poland.

Summary:
We cleaned up one car of our cattle train. Then the wounded came. One had lost his hand and had no bandage on the stump.

Vocabulary:
allotted = assigned
evidences = signs
habitable = suitable to
   live in
presently = soon

An American Woman Volunteer Escapes

We found our train—a cattle train, with evidences of its former occupants!… We managed, with the aid of an old coat and a pail of water, to make one car more habitable…. Presently the wounded came—many of them not bandaged—and thirty-two of the especially bad cases, were allotted to my car. One, who had lost his hand, had no covering on the raw stump.…

(continued on next page)

Summary:

I had no bandages, but I got a small supply. It was a sad sight for my children to see. The wounded man was patient. My children tried to comfort him.

The soldiers sang, but were interrupted by gunshots. The Germans were nearby. We got quiet.

Two more wounded were put into our car. The train started off through the bullets.

Later the babies slept in the soldier's arms. That was very touching.

Vocabulary:

agonies = severe pains

anxiety = eagerness

gauntlet = an attack
  from all sides

minor = minor scale in
  music

stolen a march = gained
  an unexpected
  advantage; sneaked
  around and appeared
  unexpectedly

I had no cotton or bandages—but I was able to get a small supply of such things.… It was a pitiful picture which my little children saw —the poor man, who had lost his hand suffering agonies from the contact of the air with the raw flesh. How it hurt, and how patient the man was—the big tears just rolling down his cheeks! I couldn't keep the children away—there was no place to send them. It was sweet to see how they tried to comfort the big soldier.…

The hours dragged by—it grew dark always the sound of battle grew nearer.… After awhile the children wanted the soldiers to sing. They began one of those weird minor melodies, singing, softly, softly.… The singing was rudely enough interrupted by the sounds of shots much nearer to us. The Germans had stolen a march and got around to the other side!… We were warned by the officer in charge to be perfectly quiet—that the train was at last to go—running the gauntlet.

At the very last moment two freshly wounded men were shoved into our car both bleeding.… The car began to move—stealing through the night.… In a few minutes we were right where the shots were flying; some of them struck our car! The bullets sang but they could not reach us—we were watched over. On through those bullets we went.

All danger was not over, but at least the bullets did not whizz about our ears. The babies were asleep, with the soldiers' arms about them —it made my heart ache to see those men— their tenderness and touching anxiety to do something.

Source: Laura de Gozdawa Turczynowicz, *When the Prussians Came to Poland: The Experiences of an American Woman during the German Invasion.* New York: G.P. Putnam's Sons, 1916.

Some Americans who had traveled in France fell in love with that country before war began. Alan Seeger (uncle of folksinger Pete Seeger) was one of those people. He was born in New York, but when France was threatened in 1914, he volunteered to help. Seeger joined the French Foreign Legion (a military unit made up of volunteers from other nations). The following is from a letter that Alan Seeger wrote to the *New York Sun* newspaper in December of 1914.

In the Trenches

Occasionally a violent fusillade to the right or left of us shows that attacks are being made and at any moment are likely to be made….

This style of warfare is extremely modern and for the artillerymen is doubtless very interesting, but for the common soldier it is anything but romantic. His role is simply to dig himself a hole in the ground and to keep hidden in it as tightly as possible. Continually under the fire of the opposing batteries, he is yet never allowed to get a glimpse of the enemy. Exposed to all the dangers of war, but with none of its enthusiasms or splendid *elan*, he is condemned to sit like an animal in its burrow and hear the shells whistle over his head and to take their little daily toll from his comrades.

Source: Alan Seeger, *Letters and Diary of Alan Seeger.* New York: Charles Scribners Sons, 1917, pp. 28-30.

Allied soldiers used periscopes to see from the trenches.

Summary:
Once in a while, shots show us that attacks are underway.

This war is modern, and perhaps interesting for artillerymen. But it isn't romantic for the common soldier. He just digs a hole and stays in it. Always under fire, he can never see the enemy. He is exposed to the dangers of war, but to none of its spirit. He is like an animal in its burrow.

Vocabulary:
artillerymen = crews of men who operate large guns
batteries = sets of guns
condemned = sentenced
continually = without stopping
elan = French for spirit and vigor
fusillade = rapid outburst; barrage

In 1914, Eric Wood was a young American architectural student working as an attaché for the American Ambassador in Paris. (An attaché is a person who does a specific job for an Ambassador. An Ambassador represents the government of another country.) Wood made four trips to the front to report back on the war. His notes describe the destruction he saw there.

Summary:

The dead were scattered around, and the wounded cried out. French soldiers hunted Germans in the forests. One German and Frenchman lay face to face, dead, each stabbed by the other's bayonet.

Vocabulary:

bayonet = blade attached
  to the muzzle of a rifle
piteous = arousing pity
squads = small military units
stragglers = those who fall
  behind
transfixed = pierced

Notes from the War Zone

The dead were scattered far and wide; and in the fields and among the grain-stacks the wounded cried out their piteous faint appeals. Little groups of German stragglers were hiding in the forests, and squads of alert French soldiers hunted them down, beating through the cover as eager setter dogs search for grouse. In one field of about six acres lay nine hundred German dead and wounded; across another, where a close-action fight had raged, two hundred French and Germans lay mixed together, all mashed and ripped. Here was the curious sight of a German and Frenchman lying face to face, both dead, and each one transfixed by the other's bayonet.

Many animals took part in the war. Horses, mules, oxen, camels, and donkeys were used to move equipment, supplies, and troops. Many ambulances were pulled through the mud by teams of horses or mules.

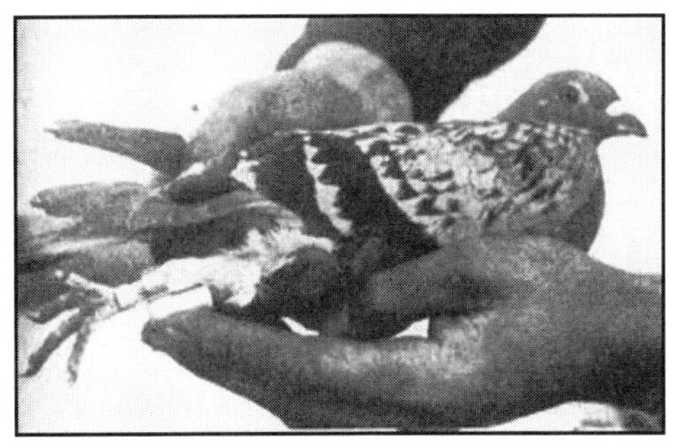

Pigeons and dogs carried messages. The pigeon shown here has a message tube fastened to its leg. Dogs guarded prisoners of war and guided soldiers blinded by gas or wounds. Like humans, these animals suffered and died from the effects of gas and other weapons.

The very birds of the air and the beasts of the field lay dead and rotting amid the general destruction. We saw feathers and bits of chickens and halves of cows. On one occasion [my driver] maintained that "it" had been a cow, while I thought "it" was a horse, and no piece large enough for certain identification could be found. Of some of the villages which had been peaceful and beautiful a week ago, there remained now only chimneys, ashes, and bits of walls rising from smouldering gray debris. A French village wrecked by battle looks very much wrecked indeed, in contrast with its habitual orderly and toy-like appearance.

I was not so horrified in viewing these ghastly sights as I had expected, because I could not put from me a sense of their unreality. The human mind is incapable of comprehending to the full such terrible happenings. One kept endlessly saying to oneself: "Can all this which we are seeing really have taken place in this once quiet French country-side, almost within the suburbs of Paris? It seems impossible— unbelievable!"

Source: Eric Fisher Wood, *The Note-Book of an Attaché: Seven Months in the War Zone.* New York: The Century Company, 1915, pp. 98-102.

Summary:
Birds and animals lay rotting. Some couldn't be identified. Some villages were now only ashes.

I wasn't as horrified as I had expected, because it all seemed so unreal. The human mind can't understand such terrible things. It seems unbelievable.

Vocabulary:
comprehending = understanding
debris = rubble; wreckage
ghastly = horrible; terrifying
habitual = usual
smouldering = burning with little smoke and no flame

New and Terrible Weapons

In World War I, science helped change the way that wars were fought. New weapons took terrible tolls on both sides. Both sides built warships that carried huge guns. German submarines cruised beneath the surface of the water, claiming both military and civilian lives. Airplanes and Airships soared overhead, spying on the enemy and dropping deadly explosives on those below. Tanks crawled along ahead of the infantry, firing huge guns from their protective metal shells. Flamethrowers destroyed buildings and humans alike. Chemical warfare was introduced, with substances that blistered, burned, and blinded soldiers. And a variety of new or improved guns appeared that had never been seen before.

Sometimes their ability to kill horrified those who did the killing. A British corporal wrote that "Our rapid fire was appalling, even to us, and the worst marksman could not miss.…" (From *The First World War,* by the Editors of *Life Magazine,* New York: Time Inc., 1964, p. 9.)

Machine guns can fire a steady stream of small ammunition. Troops charging directly at the enemy could be easily cut down by machine guns. That changed the way a war could be fought. The British developed a lightweight machine gun that was widely used in World War I. Photo above shows heavy machine gun crew.

Chemical Warfare

Both the soldier and his horse had to wear gas masks to survive.

The Germans first used poison gas in 1915—a terrible weapon that downed many French and British soldiers. Those armies were soon provided with gas masks, which made the chemicals less effective. But gas was still dangerous, as ambulance driver William Yorke Stevenson noted in his diary.

Gassed Soldiers

11 July 1916

The big bombardment was followed by a gas attack…and the fight was fierce all night…. We began to get calls around 5 a.m. and, thereafter, ran all day under heavy fire…. Nearly all the men we carried [in the ambulance] were "gassed." They kept coming in all day from the trenches, or rather shell holes…. We alone carried some twelve hundred of them, and believe me, it was some strain.

Many new dead horses along the road. The gas gets them, even the smallest whiff, and, of course, they have no masks. Even at 10 a.m. there was still enough gas to make our eyes smart. The Germans tried a new [type of shell].

(continued on next page)

Summary:

The shelling was followed by a gas attack. About 5 a.m. we started making runs for the wounded. Nearly all had been gassed. We carried 1200 of them.

There were a lot of dead horses. They had no gas masks. The next morning, there was still enough gas to make our eyes burn.

Vocabulary:

bombardment = attack with bombs or shells

Summary:

The new German shells were quiet, but spread the gas fast. The cloud of gas was about 40 feet high and 200 meters long. The men who were gassed had taken off their masks because they got sick to their stomachs or for some other reason. It isn't fun to talk to men who don't know they're soon going to die.

Vocabulary:

extended = stretched; spread out

They do not make much noise…but the gas spreads fast. [The gas cloud] was about forty feet high and extended for about two hundred meters along the Etain road. The men who were caught by it all admitted they had taken off their masks for one reason or another. Some get sick at their stomachs and that forces them to take off their masks. It is not amusing to talk to men who don't know they're good as dead!…

Source: William Yorke Stevenson, *American Ambulance, At The Front In A Flivver.* Boston & NY: Houghton Mifflin Company, 1917. Found at http://raven. cc.ukans. edu/~kansite/ww_one/memoir/stevensn.htm

In World War I, the British developed armored cars to use for observing the enemy. The cars were shielded with metal and they carried large guns. But cars with wheels often got stuck in the mud, and they couldn't cross the trenches. By 1916, Britain began producing tanks that traveled on caterpillar tracks. The new vehicles could cross both mud and trenches. The French also began building tanks, and improving on the design. These early tanks were slow, and four men were needed to steer them. But one-driver tanks that were a bit faster were very effective in the war's final battles.

Balloons and Bombs

British dirigible

Both sides used gas-filled balloons for observation. A dirigible, or steerable balloon, was invented by the French. In WWI, the British used dirigibles to hunt submarines. The Germans built more than 100 Zeppelins. These giant airships had rigid frames, like a cage on the inside. At first, Zeppelins flew higher than airplanes and above the reach of anti-aircraft guns. But those defenses were soon improved.

Powerful bombs were developed for the Zeppelins to deliver. The first massive bombing from the air was in 1915. German Zeppelins glided across the English channel and rained terror on England. Sherwood Eddy was a widely-traveled American missionary and author. In the following passage, Eddy describes a 1917 raid on London.

Bombs Fall on London

At half-past two in the morning we were awakened by the roar of the anti-aircraft guns in and around the city.... We sprang to the window and found the sky swept by a score of searchlights with their great shafts of piercing light, shooting from the dark depths of the city high into the sky, where they all converged on a single bright object that hung nine thousand feet above us. Long, and shining like silver with its flashing aluminum, the Zeppelin seemed held as if blinded by the fierce light. Bombs were dropping from it and explosions followed in rapid succession in the city beneath.

(continued on next page)

Consider this:
Note how Eddy's vivid descriptions bring the scene to life.

Vocabulary:
converged = met; came together
succession = order; one after another

Consider this:

You might try choosing a dramatic event and writing your own vivid description. Choose the best words to bring your story to life.

Vocabulary:

aeroplanes = airplanes

incendiary = something
  that causes fire

score = 20

shrapnel = metal pieces
  scattered by exploding
  shell or bomb

triumphantly = proudly
  in victory

It was a battle to the death, high in the air with all London looking on. The guns were in full play and the shell and shrapnel were bursting all about the Zeppelin…. More than a score of aeroplanes had been sent up to attack it…. The battle finally developed into a duel to the death between the machine guns of the Zeppelin and Lieutenant Robinson of the Flying Corps, who was up for two hours in his aeroplane after the enemy—one man fighting for a city of five millions. He attacked from below and bombs were thrown at his plane; then he attacked from the side as he circled about the monster, but he was driven off by their machine guns. At last, mounting high in the sky, he attacked from above. The guide-plane flashed down the signal for the guns to cease firing and give him a chance.

For a few moments all was silent; the battle seemed to be over. The great airship…was triumphantly leaving for home. Then it was that Robinson dropped his incendiary bomb. Suddenly there was an explosion. A flame of burning gas leaped into the sky. London was lit up for ten miles round about. Our room was instantly as bright as though a searchlight had flashed into the window.

Far above us was the Zeppelin in flames. Now it began to sink—first it was in a blaze of white light, then its outline turned to a dull red, finally it crumpled to a glowing cinder, sank from sight, and fell crashing to the earth. Then all was dark again. Death had fallen suddenly upon the men in the Zeppelin and upon some in the sleeping city below.

Source: Sherwood Eddy, *With Our Soldiers in France.* New York: Association Press, 1917. Found at http:// raven.cc.ukans.edu/~libsite/wwi-www/Eddy/EddyTC.htm

War Machines in the Air

Allied Breguet bomber in action.

Just 11 years after the first airplanes even got off the ground, the plane became a war machine. The little crafts made of wood and canvas weren't easy to fly. At first, pilots just went up to see what enemy ground troops were doing. Once in a while, one pilot would take a shot at another with a handgun. Then someone figured out how to fire a machine gun through the propeller without shooting the blades off—and the air war really began.

Early in WWI, pilots sometimes carried bombs in their laps and dumped them on a target. After anti-aircraft guns were in use, bombsights were invented so pilots could fly higher over targets. Fliers also learned to take off from the decks of ships with the help of catapults. Landing on a deck was much trickier, and in the early days the planes could only land nearby on the water. In 1917, the first fighter plane landed on the specially-built deck of a ship.

According to *The First World War,* by the editors of *Life Magazine*, wartime pilots didn't live very long: "The average life of an airman in late 1916 was three weeks." (New York: Time Inc., p. 36.)

There are many stories about famous flying "Aces" on both sides of the war. In 1918, American pilot Harold Buckley wrote home about a dogfight.

Commentary:

A biplane has double wings. Many WWI fighting aircraft were biplanes built of wood and canvas. A two-seater design called the Jenny Curtiss was used for training American pilots. Sopwith Camel biplane fighters were used by British flyers. Another very successful biplane fighter was the French SPAD.

WWI flyers also used some triplanes (with triple wings) and monoplanes (with the more familiar single pair of wings).

Vocabulary:

fusilage = fuselage; central body of an airplane

huddle = crouched

out-maneuvered = overcome by skillful maneuvering. Maneuvers are controlled changes in direction.

tracer = bullet that leaves a glowing or smoky trail

Dogfight

We started at 5,000 metres and it ended when he burst into flames just before he struck the ground. And what a run for my money he gave me. He really out-maneuvered me and I am convinced he had the better plane but he did not put a single bullet in my plane and his, as I afterwards found, had two or three in his engine, three in his gas tank, one right through his radiator and propeller and a goodly fat number through his wings and fusilage.

It was…a biplane having pilot and observer both having splendid machine-guns as I learned by seeing a few tracer bullets go by…. The fight lasted nearly a half hour which is awfully long, and after a little while I noticed the observer had stopped shooting for I could see the poor fellow huddle down in his cockpit every time I attacked, so then I knew he was either wounded or out of ammunition. Even after that, however, the pilot gave me an awful fight but at last I got a good burst of tracers right into his engine and he started going down in a … spinning nose dive…. He did come out, however, and I…got his gas tank. He then burst into flames, landed and tipped over. Both pilot and observer were thrown out over the top wing and to my surprise both got up and started walking. And the funny part, I don't know what made me do it, but when I saw them get up I swooped down on them and waved my hand and one of them waved back. I am glad I did not kill them but I guess I tried hard enough.

Source: Harold Buckley, *Squadron 95*. Paris: Obelisk Press, 1933; reprinted New York: Arno Press, 1972, pp. 73-5.

Submarines

American submarine (U.S. Sub L1)

German submarines—or U-boats—could stay under water only two and a half hours. But they were deadly, striking silently with torpedoes or firing deck guns from the surface. U-boats stalked the shipping lanes near England. The Germans also seeded the water with mines that exploded on contact. On his way to observe the war, U.S. Marine pilot Alfred A. Cunningham took his turn watching for underwater threats.

The Danger Zone at Sea

Sunday, November 11, 1917

S.S. "St. Paul," In danger zone

We entered the zone thickly infested with German submarines today and are still in it…I went on watch at 6 a.m. on the bridge and have been there most of the day. This morning we got a SOS call from some poor ship to the south of us saying that they were being chased by a submarine. We, of course, could not pay any attention to it. I hope he outran it. This afternoon [we] received a message that a mine field had been found directly in our course. We altered our course to the northward…. If we get through tonight, we are fairly safe.

Source: *Marine Flyer in France,* The Diary of Captain Alfred A. Cunningham, November 1917—January 1918. Graham A. Cosmas, Editor. Found at http://raven.cc.ukans. edu/~kansite/ww_one/marines/cunning/flyer.html

Commentary:

The *St. Paul* was a passenger ship, which had some women and children on board. But at this point in the war, German U-boats were trying to sink civilian ships as well as military ones. Of course, a mine explodes when hit by any kind of vessel.

Vocabulary:

altered = changed

infested = overrun with large numbers of something

America Moves toward War

As the war raged on in Europe, it seemed far away to most Americans. From the first, the United States had refused to take sides, remaining neutral. But some events began to turn American opinion against Germany. Gradually, the U.S. was pushed toward joining the war on the side of the Allies.

Germany Invades a Neutral Country

The country of Belgium also remained neutral. But Germany's plan of conquest called for the early defeat of Belgium. When Germany invaded the neutral country in 1914, the whole world was shocked. And neutral America didn't feel so far removed from the conflict.

U-boats Sink a Passenger Ship

At first, German submarines only attacked warships. But in 1915, the Germans declared they would also go after merchant ships. Then, a German U-boat sank the British passenger liner *Lusitania*, sending over 1,000 people to their death in the sea. Included among the dead were 128 Americans. After this sinking, the Germans stopped attacking non-military ships.

Consider this:

A warning from the German Embassy was printed in major New York newspapers on the day the *Lusitania* left, prior to its departure. Yet, no passengers cancelled their plans. *Lusitania* Captain William Turner laughed and dismissed the German threat. The ship was torpedoed off the Irish coast on May 7th.

The attack on the *Lusitania* brought more pressure on the U.S. to enter the war, and President Woodrow Wilson demanded a policy of "strict accountability."

NOTICE!

TRAVELLERS intending to embark on the Atlantic voyage are reminded that a state of war exists between Germany and her allies and Great Britain and her allies; that the zone of war includes the waters adjacent to the British Isles; that, in accordance with formal notice given by the Imperial German Government, vessels flying the flag of Great Britain, or of any of her allies, are liable to destruction in those waters and that travellers sailing in the war zone on ships of Great Britain or her allies do so at their own risk.

IMPERIAL GERMAN EMBASSY
WASHINGTON D. C., APRIL 22, 1915.

Pacifism

Some Americans continued to object to making any move toward war. A small group of church leaders called for pacifism. Pacifism is the belief that disputes between nations can be—and should be—settled peacefully. Pacifists are opposed to using violence to solve problems. They often refuse to serve in the military, or ask to serve in non-fighting jobs such as medical units.

John Haynes Holmes was a Unitarian clergyman and a pacifist. He believed that war was caused by cut-throat economic competition among nations. The following excerpts are from his 1916 statement on "radical pacifism." (Radical means extreme.)

Radical Pacifism

If you look upon America as a great ideal of the spirit, independent of territory and population and wealth, then all such things as armies and navies become matters of supreme indifference. For the spirit is impregnable to all the attacks that the hand of man can bring against it…. What if Germany came here today as she came to Belgium yesterday! …No conqueror that has ever lived could destroy the sense of brotherhood that is at the heart of our American life: no sword that was ever forged could smite the love of democracy which is the impulse of our civilization. A free people would still be free, even though in chains—and a valiant spirit still survive, even the hour of death….

To all such attacks as these, the soul of America is impregnable. But there is another kind of attack, which may well be feared by all those who love this nation not for what she has, but for what she is. I refer to the attack not upon her soil but upon her soul—an attack which is

(continued on next page)

Summary:

If you think of America's spirit, rather than its territory or people, war becomes unimportant. Brotherhood can't be conquered. Love of democracy can't be destroyed by the sword. Free people remain free in chains, and even at death. America cannot be beaten by physical attacks. But there is another kind to be feared—attacks on her soul.

Vocabulary:

forged = made; formed by heat

impregnable = impossible to take by force

impulse = motivating force

independent = separate from

indifference = having no feeling for or against something

valiant = brave; noble

Summary:

Some want America to abandon her ideals and follow the sad example of history. Those people are our real foes. If we do that, we will no longer be a people of ideas. We will be people of wealth and power, who measure their greatness by land or money and not by the ideals of their spirit.

To keep America's ideals—to preserve her soul—is our highest duty.

Vocabulary:

conducted = carried out
fraternity = brotherhood
inviolate = intact;
   undamaged
melancholy = unhappy;
   sad
treacherous = dangerous;
   untrustworthy
trodden = well-traveled

now being conducted all along the line by those who…would have America abandon her priceless ideals of brotherhood and democracy, and follow the melancholy example of the great empires of history…. Our real foes are of our own household—those men who, from motives however worthy, would lead America out of the trodden paths of fraternity and peace, into the treacherous ways of blood and iron. [If that happens…] No longer shall we be a people of ideas. On the contrary, we shall be a people of wealth, power, dominion, glory—a people who measure their greatness by the territory they occupy or the trade they own, and not by the ideals of the spirit which they serve….

To keep America faithful to her ideals—to help her at this crisis of temptation, to preserve her soul inviolate—this is the highest duty of the present hour….

Source: John Haynes Holmes, *New Wars for Old: Being a Statement of Radical Pacifism in Terms of Force Versus Non-Resistance, with Special Reference to the Facts and Problems of the Great War*. New York: Dodd, Mead and Company, 1916, pp. 345-48.

The Zimmermann Telegram

In November of 1916, the British intercepted a telegram that turned out to be very important to the United States. The message was from a German diplomat named Arthur Zimmermann. It was sent to the German Minister to Mexico, named von Eckhardt.

It was in code #13040, which the Germans thought was unbreakable. But the British had had the code book on #13040 since 1915 and were able to read the message. Afraid that Americans would consider it a fake, they moved slowly. In February of 1917, they finally took the decoded message to President Wilson.

A reproduction of the original coded telegram appears below.

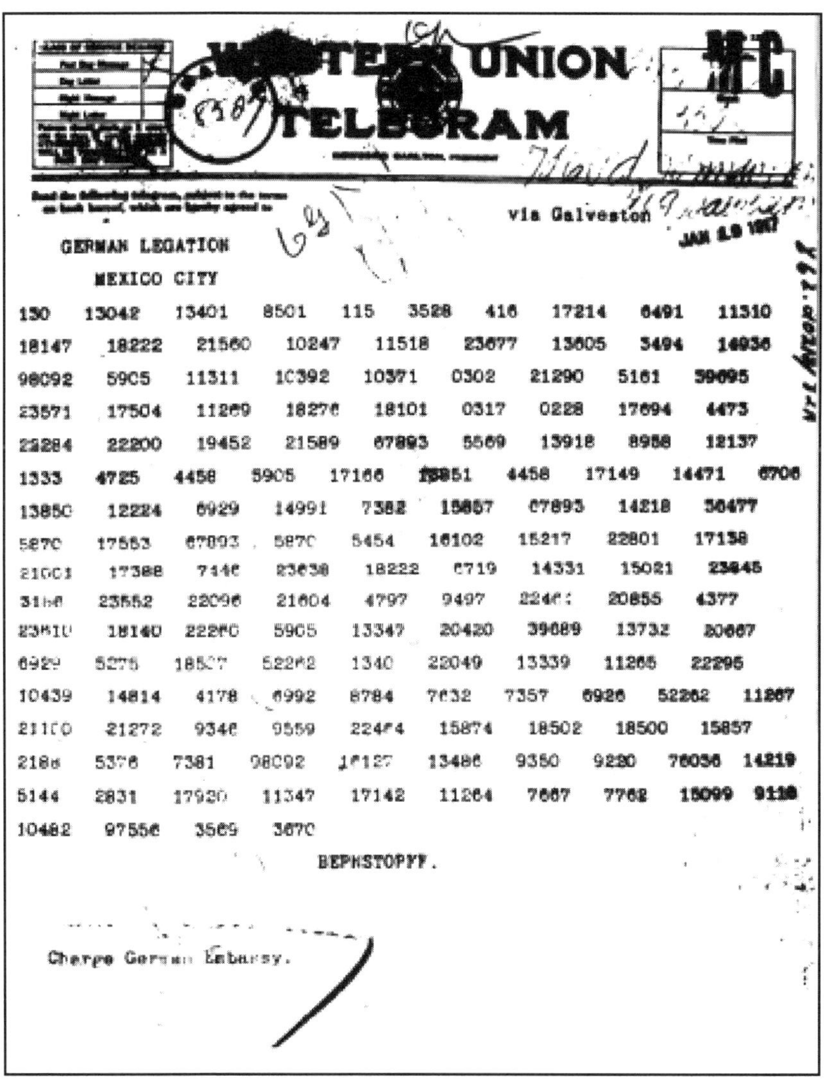

The Message

Zimmermann's message invited Mexico to enter the war against the Allies. In return, Germany promised that after the war was won, they would return Mexican lands that the United States had taken away in the 1846-1848 war with Mexico. Those lands included Arizona, New Mexico, and Texas!

President Wilson apparently accepted the telegraph as real. But when the story was published in newspapers on March 1, many Americans thought it was a fake. Then—for unknown reasons—Zimmermann himself announced that the message was real. Americans were furious, and objections to entering the war began to fade.

Below is the decoded message.

TELEGRAM RECEIVED.

FROM 2nd from London # 5747.

"We intend to begin on the first of February unrestricted submarine warfare. We shall endeavor in spite of this to keep the United States of America neutral. In the event of this not succeeding, we make Mexico a proposal of alliance on the following basis: make war together, make peace together, generous financial support and an understanding on our part that Mexico is to reconquer the lost territory in Texas, New Mexico, and Arizona. The settlement in detail is left to you. You will inform the President of the above most secretly as soon as the outbreak of war with the United States of America is certain and add the suggestion that he should, on his own initiative, invite Japan to immediate adherence and at the same time mediate between Japan and ourselves. Please call the President's attention to the fact that the ruthless employment of our submarines now offers the prospect of compelling England in a few months to make peace." Signed, ZIMMERMANN.

Rumors and Reports of Cruelty

Many stories were told about German cruelty to the people they conquered. Some of these were doubtless just rumors, and others true. These stories helped convince Americans that they should enter the war against Germany.

Herbert Clark Hoover (later the 31st president of the United States) was made head of the Commission for Relief in Belgium. He visited the conquered country, and reported back on conditions there. In 1917 he wrote the following letter, calling for Americans to join the battle.

Herbert Hoover on Belgium

September, 1917

I have been often called upon for a statement of my observation of German rule in Belgium and Northern France.

I have neither the desire nor the adequate pen to picture the scenes which have heated my blood through the two and a half years that I have spent in work for the relief of these 10,000,000 people.

The sight of the destroyed homes and cities, the widowed and fatherless, the destitute, the physical misery of a people but partially nourished at best, the deportation of men by tens of thousands to slavery in German mines and factories, the execution of men and women for paltry effusions of their loyalty to their country, the sacking of every resource through financial robbery, the fattening of armies on the slender produce of the country, the denudation of the country of cattle, horses, and textiles; all these

(continued on next page)

Summary:

I'm often asked to tell what I saw in German-ruled Belgium and France.

I haven't the heart or words to picture it. It has made me angry for two and a half years.

The things we saw: destroyed homes and cities, miserable people, men sent into slavery, executions for loyalty to their country, taking of animals and goods.

Vocabulary:

adequate = sufficient
denudation = stripping
  bare
deportation = being
  expelled from a country
destitute = lacking
  everything; poverty-
  stricken
effusions = outpourings
  of feeling

Summary:
We had to witness without helping. These scenes are not caused by battle madness, but by a race wanting to rule the world.

The world knows all this, but they can never know the agony of the people who have felt every emotion. And why? Because they stood in the way of autocracy.

I believe that if we don't fight now, all these things may happen to us. But even if the Atlantic protects us, remember Belgium. Can we live in a world where such people are trampled and not fight back?

Vocabulary:
agony = severe pain
autocracy = rule by a
　　single person with
　　unlimited power
gamut = range

things we had to witness, dumb to help other than by protest and sympathy, during this long and terrible time—and still these are not the events of battle heat, but the effects of a grinding heel of a race demanding the mastership of the world.

All these things are well known to the world —but what can never be known is the dumb agony of the people, the expressionless faces of millions whose souls have passed the whole gamut of emotions. And why? Because these, a free and democratic people, dared to plunge their bodies before the march of autocracy.

I myself believe that if we do not fight and fight now, all these things are possible to us— but even should the broad Atlantic prove our present defender, there is still Belgium. Is it worth while for us to live in a world where this free and unoffending people is to be trampled into the earth and to raise no sword in protest?

Source: Dana C. Munro, ed., *German War Practices.* Washington: The Committee on Public Information, 1917, pp. 81-2.

U-boats Will Again Attack Civilians

There had been international protest over the sinking of the *Lusitania.* In April of 1916, Germany had announced that its submarines would no longer attack any and all ships at sea.

However, on February 1, 1917, Germany again announced a change. They would now use U-boats to attack any ships they found on the way to or from ports in nations unfriendly to Germany. Once again, all ships—including commercial vessels and passenger liners—could be sunk. This included the ships of neutral nations such as the United States.

President Wilson Calls for War

President Wilson had kept hoping that peace was possible. But after the German announcement that it would again attack civilian ships, the U.S. broke off diplomatic relations with Germany. Then Wilson was given the Zimmermann telegram in February. For Wilson and many other Americans, neutrality was at an end.

President Wilson called a Joint Session of Congress on April 2, 1917. He said that Germany's action was, in essence, a declaration of war against the United States. Following are excerpts from the speech, in which President Wilson called upon Congress to declare war.

The President Speaks to Congress

I have called the Congress into extraordinary session because there are serious, very serious, choices of policy to be made, and made immediately, which it was neither right nor constitutionally permissible that I should assume the responsibility of making.

On the 3rd of February last, I officially laid before you the extraordinary announcement of the Imperial German government that on and after the 1st day of February it was its purpose to put aside all restraints of law or of humanity and use its submarines to sink every vessel that sought to approach either the ports of Great Britain and Ireland or the western coasts of Europe or any of the ports controlled by the enemies of Germany within the Mediterranean.

. . . .

(continued on next page)

Summary:

I have called Congress because there are serious choices to be made, and right away. It is neither right nor legal for me to make them.

Last February, I told you of the German decision to use submarines to sink any ship approaching any port controlled by the enemies of Germany.

Vocabulary:

assume = take on

constitutionally permissible = legal according to the U.S. Constitution

extraordinary = unusual; amazing

policy = official plans of action

restraints = limitations

Summary:

I have a deep sense of the sadness of this step, but it is my duty. I advise Congress to declare Germany's action to be nothing less than war against the U.S. Congress should accept this and take steps to ready our defenses and exert our power to beat Germany and end the war.

We don't blame the German people for this war. Their government acted without their approval.

The German government means to stir up enemies, as the [Zimmermann telegram] shows.

The world must be made safe for democracy. We don't want to rule, but to make the rights of mankind secure.

Vocabulary:

belligerent = one that is
  at war
deem = judge
eloquent = vivid
impulse = urging
intercepted = captured;
  caught
profound = deep

With a profound sense of the solemn and even tragical character of the step I am taking and of the grave responsibilities which it involves, but in unhesitating obedience to what I deem my constitutional duty, I advise that the Congress declare the recent course of the Imperial German Government to be in fact nothing less than war against the government and people of the United States; that it formally accept the status of belligerent which has thus been thrust upon it; and that it take immediate steps, not only to put the country in a more thorough state of defense but also to exert all its power and employ all its resources to bring the government of the German Empire to terms and end the war.

. . . .

We have no quarrel with the German people. We have no feeling toward them but one of sympathy and friendship. It was not upon their impulse that their government acted in entering this war. It was not with their previous knowledge or approval….

. . . .

[That German government] means to stir up enemies against us at our very doors, the intercepted note to the German minister at Mexico is eloquent evidence.

. . . .

The world must be made safe for democracy. Its peace must be planted upon the tested foundations of political liberty. We have no selfish ends to serve. We desire no conquest, no dominion…. We are but one of the champions of the rights of mankind. We shall be satisfied when those rights have been made as secure as the faith and the freedom of nations can make them.

. . . .

There are, it may be, many months of fiery trial and sacrifice ahead of us. It is a fearful thing to lead this great peaceful people into war, into the most terrible and disastrous of all wars, civilization itself seeming to be in the balance. But the right is more precious than peace, and we shall fight for the things which we have always carried nearest our hearts—for democracy, for the right of those who submit to authority to have a voice in their own governments, for the rights and liberties of small nations, for a universal dominion of right by such a concert of free peoples as shall bring peace and safety to all nations and make the world itself at last free.

To such a task we can dedicate our lives and our fortunes, everything that we are and everything that we have, with the pride of those who know that the day has come when America is privileged to spend her blood and her might for the principles that gave her birth and happiness and the peace which she has treasured. God helping her, she can do no other.

Source: 65 Congress, 1 Session, Senate Document No. 5, quoted in *1916-1918: World War and Prosperity*, vol. 14 of *The Annals of America*. Chicago and other cities: Encyclopedia Britannica, Inc., 1968, pp. 77-82.

Summary:
There may be months of sacrifice ahead. It is terrible to lead peaceful people into this war. But civilization is at risk. The right is more valuable than peace. We shall fight for democracy. Free people together shall bring peace and safety to all, and make the world free.

We can dedicate everything to such a task.

Commentary:
This echoes the 1776 Declaration of Independence, which ends with: "we mutually pledge to each other our lives, our Fortunes, and our sacred Honor."

Vocabulary:
concert = unlty
dedicate = commit
disastrous = causing great misfortune
dominion = control; rule
principles = basic truths
submit = give in

America Declares War

On April 6, 1917, Congress officially declared war against Germany. Americans were going to Europe to fight for democracy and bring peace to the world. Like the Allies in Europe, many Americans believed that this war would end all wars.

Recruiting poster, encouraging young men to insure the safety of America. (Library of Congress)

Raising a Military Force

When war was declared, the U.S. military wasn't nearly large enough to do the job. The Selective Service Act of 1917 created an agency to draft young men into service. Men also volunteered in large numbers. Over the next year, the military grew from about 200,000 men to more than 4 million.

Local draft boards were set up to select those who would serve in the military. Those with large families, jobs in important industries, agriculture, or in other essential industries could be exempted (excused) from being drafted.

Convincing the Public

The United States had been neutral for more than three years. Now many Americans still had to be convinced that going to war was the right thing. In April 1917, President Woodrow Wilson set up a committee to do just that.

The Committee on Public Information (CPI) had the job of telling the public about the war—and getting them to support it. Journalist George Creel was made chairman of CPI. He hired writers, artists, Hollywood producers, and movie stars such as Mary Pickford, Douglas Fairbanks, Charlie Chaplin, and Norma Talmadge. The stars and other well-known citizens spoke out for patriotism. Creel said that 150,000 men and women helped with the committee's work.

The CPI published pamphlets, magazines, newspapers, and posters. They produced movies and planned war exhibits for state fairs. The committee also kept check on everything about the war that the public might see, hear, or read. They convinced the American press to voluntarily censor what they published for the safety of American soldiers.

After the war ended, George Creel wrote a book explaining what the CPI had done, and why. Following are excerpts from Creel's book.

The CPI at Work

The printed word, the spoken word, the motion picture, the telegraph, the cable, the wireless, the poster, the signboard—all these were used in our campaign to make our own people and all other peoples understand the causes that compelled America to take arms....

...What we had to have was no mere surface unity, but a passionate belief in the justice of America's cause that should weld the people of the United States into one white-hot mass instinct with fraternity, devotion, courage, and deathless determination. The *warwill*, the will-to-win, of a democracy depends upon the degree to which each one of all the people of that democracy can concentrate and consecrate body and soul and spirit in the supreme effort of service and sacrifice. What had to be driven home was that all business was the nation's business, and every task a common task for a single purpose.

As swiftly as might be, there were put into pamphlet form America's reasons for entering the war, the meaning of America, the nature of our free institutions, our war aims, likewise analyses of the Prussian system, the purposes of the imperial German government, and full exposure of the enemy's misrepresentations, aggressions, and barbarities....

Source: George Creel, *How We Advertised America.* New York: Harper & Brothers, 1920, pp. 5-8.

Invasion…in the Imagination

The CPI's propaganda posters and pamphlets (booklets) were very success-ful. A professor of English at Stanford University put his imagination to work for the CPI. To help convince Americans that they must back the war effort, John S. P. Tatlock explained what it would be like if the Germans invaded New Jersey. Following are excerpts from his pamphlet.

If the Germans Invaded New Jersey…

[A German attack would be] sudden, because their settled way is always to attack suddenly. …One body of from 50,000 to 100,000 men lands, let us suppose, at Barnegat Bay, New Jersey, and advances without meeting resistance, for the brave but small American army is scattered elsewhere…. They first demand wine for the officers and beer for the men. Angered to find that an American town does not contain large quantities of either, they pillage and burn the post office and most of the hotels and stores. Then they demand $1,000,000 from the residents. One feeble old woman tries to conceal $20 which she has been hoarding in her desk drawer; she is taken out and hanged (to save a cartridge). Some of the teachers in two district schools meet a fate which makes them envy her. The Catholic priest and Methodist minister are thrown into a pig-sty, while the German soldiers look on and laugh. Some of the officers quarter themselves in a handsome house on the edge of town, insult the ladies of the family, and destroy and defile the contents of the house. By this time some of the soldiers have managed to get drunk; one of them discharges his gun accidentally, the cry goes up that the residents are firing on the troops, and then hell breaks loose. Robbery, murder and outrage run riot. Fifty leading citizens are lined up against the First National Bank building, and shot. Most of the town and the beautiful pinewoods are burned, and then the troops move on….

Source: John S. P. Tatlock, "Why America Fights Germany," Washington: Committee on Public Information (pamphlet), March 1918. Quoted in James R. Mock and Cedric Larson, *Words that Won the War: The Story of the Committee on Public Information*. Princeton: Princeton University Press, 1939, pp. 166-67.

Tom Swift and his War Tank, or Doing His Bit for
Uncle Sam *was the 21st book in the popular series
about a young American inventor. In this book and the
one that followed it*—Tom Swift and his Air Scout,
or Uncle Sam's Mastery of the Sky—*Tom does his
part for the war effort.*

Tom Swift Does His Part

The first book about Tom Swift, a fictional young American inventor and
adventurer, first appeared in 1910. The series became very popular, and 40
novels were published between 1910 and 1941. Several different authors wrote
them, all using the name Victor Appleton.

In *Tom Swift and his War Tank, or Doing His Bit for Uncle Sam,* America has
entered the Great War. The young inventor hasn't been drafted, and he doesn't
explain to anybody why he hasn't voluntarily enlisted for military service.

Friends begin to wonder if he is a "slacker" who is trying to stay out of the war. It turns out, of course, that Tom is hard at work inventing a new and better tank for the American forces. The following excerpt is taken from a conversation with friends about how each person can help out.

Consider this:

What ideas is the author trying to get across to the reader in this fictional conversation?

Vocabulary:

exempted = excused from an obligation to which others are subject

Jove = name used as a mild oath; Jupiter, the highest god in Roman mythology

"We've got to do our bit…"

"Everybody who has a part in it—whether he fights as a soldier or only knits like the Red Cross girls—will be telling about it for years after," went on the girl, and she looked at Tom eagerly.

"Yes," he agreed. "…A lot of our men have been called. We tried to have some of them exempted, and did manage it in a few cases."

"You did?" cried Mr. Nestor, as if in surprise. "You stopped men from going to war!"

"Only so they could work on airship motors for the Government," Tom quietly explained.

"Oh! Well, of course, that's part of the game," agreed Mary's father. "A lot more of our boys are going off next week. Doesn't it make you thrill, Tom, when you see them marching off, even if they haven't their uniforms yet? Jove, if I wasn't too old, I'd go in a minute!"

"Father!" cried Mary.

"Yes, I would!" he declared. "The German government has got to be beaten, and we've got to do our bit; everybody has—man, woman and child!"

"Yes," agreed Tom, in a low voice, "that's very true. But every one, in a sense, has to judge for himself what the 'bit' is. We can't all do the same."

Source: Victor Appleton, *Tom Swift and his War Tank, or Doing His Bit for Uncle Sam*. New York, Grosset & Dunlap, in cooperation with the Stratemeyer Syndicate, 1918.

American Troops Go to War

Major General John J. Pershing was put in command of the American Expeditionary Force. In June of 1917, the first American troops were shipped to France. It would be another year before large numbers of U.S. soldiers arrived.

The American troops were in a land strange to most of them, fighting a war like none the world had seen before. They had little time to adjust. They were quickly plunged into the same horrors the Allied troops had suffered for more than three years. Americans arrived late in the war, but they made a difference. The new troops turned the tide against the Germans.

American soldiers grab a quick bite to eat in their trench.

Doughboys

American soldiers—especially the infantry—were called Doughboys. Infantry soldiers are those who march and fight on foot.

In the American colonies, the word doughboy referred to a baker's apprentice. In Europe, fried flour dumplings—sort of an early form of doughnut—were called doughboys. But no one knows exactly how the word got connected to the military. "Doughboy" was first used for U.S. infantry in the 1846-48 war with Mexico. It also turns up in first-hand accounts from the Civil War—sometimes mockingly. In World War I, doughboy became a popular nickname for all American troops in Europe, not just the infantry. After that war, the term wasn't used as much.

Source: Information above is from Michael E. Hanlon, "The Origins of Doughboy," on the web page "The Story of the American Expeditionary Forces" at http://www.worldwar1.com/dbc/origindb.htm

Black infantrymen in Alsace, France, 1918 (National Archives). *African Americans were drafted in higher percentages than white men, and were given fewer exemptions for families or jobs. There were practically no African Americans on the draft boards. Black soldiers were kept segregated in all-black units and denied promotion to officers. Nevertheless, many African Americans volunteered for duty. Their courage in combat earned them high praise.*

Notes from the Front

Those involved in the war kept all kinds of records, from personal diaries and letters to official reports. These give us a glimpse of what the war was like for Americans.

Captain Alfred A. Cunningham was the first U.S. Marine Corps aviator. After the United States formally declared war on Germany, Cunningham was sent to Europe to observe the Allied forces in France. He found "an unusual number of Americans here learning to fly for the French Flying Corps." Excerpts from his report follow.

An American Flyer in a French Plane

Tuesday, December 18, 1917

Got up frozen stiff. The weather fairly clear. Persuaded a French pilot of a biplane fighting Spad to take me over the lines. We went up like an elevator and talk about speed! We were over the lines in no time and I was all eyes…. I saw something to one side that looked like a fountain of red ink. Found it was the machine gun tracer bullets from the ground.…..

At about 8 p.m. we were huddled around a small fire in the hut when we heard 3 boche machines fly over very low. Two of them did not locate our place and went on. We went outside and saw the other 1 flying around trying to locate the hangars so we made for the machine gun pit. He finally flew down the line and let go a couple of bombs, as he came over we opened on him but the gun jammed and no one could fix it in the dark. He made 3 trips and let go 2 bombs each trip. Then he left us…. We went back and tried to sleep but every time a big gun would go off I thought it was another raid. I am writing this Wednesday night with my hands blue from cold. There is certainly no lack of excitement around here.

Source: *Marine Flyer in France,* The Diary of Captain Alfred A. Cunningham, November 1917—January 1918. Graham A. Cosmas, editor. Found at http://raven.cc.ukans. edu/~kansite/ww_one/marines/cunning/flyer.html

Commentary:

After this tour, Cunningham went back to the U.S. and worked out plans for American flyers to enter the combat.

Vocabulary:

biplane = a plane with
   double wings
boche = German
tracer = bullet that leaves
   a glowing or smoky trail
Spad = French fighter
   plane used in WWI

J. F. Oakleaf was an infantry Captain in France from May, 1918 to the end of the war in August. His notes on the war were published in 1921 for a reunion of the company he served with.

Summary:

Later we would have thought where we lived was all right, but at first it was a shock to be put in barns and chicken coops.

We had classes in weapons and other subjects. Many of these things could only be learned from men who had been in the fighting.

We received British equipment, gas masks, and helmets. The masks had been tested.

At first, we had trouble with the British food ration. There wasn't enough food to keep us in shape.

There was no coffee. We learned to drink tea. Later, we complained so much that we got coffee.

Vocabulary:

billeting = lodging for
   troops
habitual = by force of habit
ration = food issued to
   military
sufficient = enough

New Experiences

May, 1918.

The regiment marched to its billeting area. … Judging from later experiences this billeting area would be called fair, but to green troops straight from our well regulated camps in the States, it was a great source of disappointment to take up living quarters in French barns, lofts and chicken coops.…

Schools were started in all branches of the military game, such as for the Lewis gun, bayonet work, gas mask drill, hand and rifle grenades, intelligence and the like. There were also lectures on these subjects given by the British Officers to both our officers and men.… Many of these points were such as could only be learned by direct contact with men who had been in the fighting themselves.…

We began to receive British equipment.… We were also provided with gas masks and helmets, the former being tested on the men in a gas chamber while in this area.…

During these early days we were having a hard struggle with the British Ration …

The difficulty experienced was not due to lack of quality; the quantity, however, was of such serious shortage that every one felt that our men were not getting sufficient food to keep them in working condition.…

There was no coffee, (perhaps the greatest hardship of all to the American doughboy), although as time went on we became quite habitual tea drinkers. Later, after many bitter complaints, we received a regular coffee issue.…

29th October, 1918

During the whole day of September 28th visibility was fair, it rained during the morning. Our front line trenches were subject to considerable machine gun fire and the roads used by transports subject to shell fire all day....

[When U.S. and Allied troops attacked] ... visibility became poor, due to unfavorable atmospheric conditions and our smoke screen to cover our advance. It was difficult to see more than a few yards because a heavy fog hung close to the ground. Advance was then made by compass reading and as orderly as possible under an enemy counter barrage, the first wave suffered many casualties during the initial advance....

The advance was then continued with little resistance until the remaining troops arrived at the first wire entanglements of the Hindenburg Line. At this point they met the full resistance of a fortified position such as the world had never known. However by desperate fighting and on account of the fact that our tremendous barrage had opened devious ways through acres of barbed wire, portions of our 2nd Battalion were able to establish themselves.... The position was held against severe counter attacks... until reinforced by troops of the 3rd Australian Division at 1030 hour. After which our troops aided the Australian troops in cleaning up many enemy machine gun nests in that vicinity....

. . . .

The tanks assigned to us in this attack were put out of action shortly after the zero hour...as it afterwards proved they were good targets on the skyline for the enemy artillery, practically no assistance in wiping out machine gun nests was rendered by the tanks.

(continued on next page)

Summary:

It had rained, but during the day, visibility was fair. Our frontline trenches and the roads were fired on all day.

When our troops attacked, we couldn't see well because our own smoke screen mixed with a heavy fog. We used a compass to move ahead. We were under fire and had many casualties.

We advanced, and met terrible resistance. We fought through broken barbed wire and held our position against counter-attacks until Australian reinforcements arrived. Then we cleaned out the enemy machine guns.

Our tanks didn't help because they made good targets.

Vocabulary:

atmospheric = air or climate in a specific place
barrage = heavy curtain of artillery fire
devious = not straightforward; shifty
fortified = protected
reinforced = strengthened
rendered = made
subject = exposed to; likely to receive
vicinity = nearby area
visibility = greatest distance to which it is possible to see

At Regimental Headquarters special attention was given to assemble all stragglers and slightly wounded soldiers who had received medical attention, these reporting to a sergeant who replaced any lost equipment, enabling them to be returned to the forward positions, carrying with them boxes of hand grenades....

Source: J.F. Oakleaf, *Notes on the Operations of the 108th Infantry Overseas.* Printed for the first Reunion of Company "I" 108th Infantry, U. S. A., Olean Times Publishing Company, April 13th, 1921. Found at http://raven.cc.ukans.edu/~kansite/ww_one/memoir/Oakleaf/108th.htm

American Heroes

The Alvin C. York stamp was issued in 2000.

There were heroes from all countries and on both sides of the brutal WWI battlefields. Captain Eddie Rickenbacker—who shot down 26 German planes—was America's best known flying ace.

Among those who won the Medal of Honor for bravery in the war, the most famous is probably Sgt. Alvin C. York. Due to his religion, York was originally a conscientious objector (a person who won't fight for religious reasons). But because his religious sect was not well-known, he was drafted anyhow. When his patrol was attacked, York picked off 20 German soldiers and forced the rest to surrender. He returned to the American lines with 132 prisoners.

Songwriters and Soldier Poets

Americans—both soldiers and those at home—naturally found ways to express their feelings about the war. Popular songwriter Irving Berlin was drafted and put to work creating shows to entertain troops who were training for war. Berlin's Doughboy Review included numbers such as this one:

Oh How I Hate To Get Up in the Morning!
by Irving Berlin

Oh! how I hate to get up in the
   morning,
Oh! how I'd love to remain in bed;
For the hardest blow of all,
   Is to hear the bugler call:
You've got to get up,
   You've got to get up this
     morning!

Some day I'm going to murder the
   bugler,
Some day they're going to find him
   dead;
I'll amputate his reville,
   And step upon it heavily,
And spend the rest of my life in
   bed.

As America went to war, perhaps the most famous song was "Over There."

Over There
by George M. Cohan

Over There, Over There
Send the word, send the word,
  Over There
That the Yanks are coming,
  The Yanks are coming,
The drums rum tumming everywhere
So prepare, Say a Prayer
Send the word, send the word to beware
We'll be over, we're coming over.
And we won't be back till it's over
  Over there!

Source: Songs found in "Doughboy Music" on website
"The Story of the American Expeditionary Forces" at
http://www.worldwar1.com/dbc/music.htm

Alan Seeger

Alan Seeger was an American who volunteered for the French Foreign Legion. In his poem "I Have a Rendevouz with Death," Seeger seems to foresee his own fate. He was killed in France in July of 1916, in an assault on a German trench. Following is an abridged version of his poem.

I Have a Rendevouz with Death

I have a rendevouz with Death
At some disputed barricade,
When Spring comes back with rustling shade
And apple-blossoms fill the air—
I have a rendevouz with Death
When Spring brings back blue days and fair.
It may be he shall take my hand
And lead me into his dark land
And close my eyes and quench my breath—
It may be I shall pass him still.
On some scarred slope of battered hill,
When Spring comes round his year
And the first meadow-flowers appear.
God knows 'twere better to be deep
Pillowed in silk and scented down,
Where Love throbs out in blissful sleep,
Pulse nigh to pulse, and breath to breath,
Where hushed awakenings are dear....
But I've a rendevouz with Death
At midnight in some flaming town,
When Spring trips north again this year,
And I to my pledged word am true,
I shall not fail that rendevouz.

Source: Alan Seeger, *Poems By Alan Seeger.*
New York: Charles Scribners Son's, 1920, p. 144.

Joyce Kilmer

When he went to war, Joyce Kilmer was already well-known for his poetry. The most famous is "Trees," but critics especially praise his war poems. Kilmer was killed by a sniper's bullet while on patrol, July 30, 1918.

Rouge Bouquet

In a wood they call the Rouge Bouquet
There is a new made grave today,
Built by never a spade nor pick
Yet covered with earth ten meters thick,
There lie many fighting men,
Dead in their youthful prime,
Never to laugh nor love again
Nor taste the summertime.
For death came flying through the air
And stopped his flight at the dugout stair
Touched his prey and left them there
Clay to Clay.
He hid their bodies stealthily
In the soil of the land they fought to free
And fled away.
Now over the grave abrupt and clear
Three volleys ring,
And perhaps their brave young spirits hear.

Source: Joyce Kilmer, from "Doughboy Verse," on website "The Story of the American Expeditionary Forces" at http://www.worldwar1.com/dbc/ dbverse.htm#12

Archibald MacLeish

Captain Archibald MacLeish was an ambulance driver and artilleryman. His brother Kenneth, a navy flyer, was killed in the war. Archibald MacLeish won a Pulitizer Prize for his poetry in 1933, and again in 1958 for *J.B.: A Play in Verse.* He was appointed Librarian of Congress in 1939.

In his poem "The Silent Slain," Macleish echoes "The Song of Roland," a medieval French song. Roland leads 20,000 men into an ambush at the pass of Roncevalles (Roncevaux). Begged to sound his horn and recall his men, Roland refuses and many men are killed. When only 60 are left alive, Roland finally sounds the horn. The third blast cracks the horn and bursts the veins in Roland's own neck. It's too late to save anyone, and all die on the battlefield. The French phrase refers to the "long breath" of the horn.

The Silent Slain

We too, we too, descending once again
The hills of our own land, we too have heard
Far off — Ah, que ce cor a longue haleine —
The horn of Roland in the passages of Spain,
The first, the second blast, the failing third,
And with the third turned back and climbed once more
The steep road southward, and heard faint the sound
Of swords, of horses, the disastrous war,
And crossed the dark defile at last, and found
At Roncevaux upon the darkening plain
The dead against the dead and on the silent ground
The silent slain —

Source: Archibald MacLeish, from ""Doughboy Verse," on website "The Story of the American Expeditionary Forces" at http://www.worldwar1.com/dbc/dbverse.htm#12

Afterword: The Great War Ends

On November 10, 1918, the Great War was over. An armistice was declared and the fighting stopped. (An armistice is a truce, a halt to fighting.) Figures vary, but according to some sources, the Allies had lost more than 4,888,000 men in battle. More than 12,800,000 were wounded, and more than 3,000,000 civilians had been killed.

The Central Powers suffered more than 3,000,000 military deaths, more than 8,400,000 wounded, and more than 3,485,000 civilian deaths.

Of the American Doughboys, 52,947 were killed in battle or died from wounds. Even more died from influenza and accidents. The total of American dead was 125,000.

Most doughboys were sent home right away. Those who were assigned to occupation duty in Europe finally left in 1923.

A Lasting Peace?

After the war, the victorious Allies were torn between two goals. Some simply wanted to punish the defeated Central Powers. Others still believed that this had been the "war to end all wars." They hoped that lessons learned in the Great War would lead to a lasting peace.

Several world leaders had discussed forming an international organization to help prevent future wars. American President Woodrow Wilson included the idea in his Fourteen Points, which called for cooperation and respect between nations. The principles of the Fourteen Points are listed below.

The Fourteen Points

1. Open covenants of peace, openly arrived at

2. Absolute freedom of navigation upon the seas

3. The removal...of all economic barriers and the establishment of an equality of trade conditions among...nations...

4. ...national armaments will be reduced to the lowest point consistent with domestic safety

5. ...impartial adjustment of all colonial claims

6. ...evacuation of all Russian territory...

7. Belgium...must be evacuated and restored....

8. All French territory should be freed and the invaded portions restored....

9. A readjustment of the frontiers of Italy...

10. The peoples of Austria-Hungary...should be accorded the freest opportunity of autonomous development.

11. Rumania, Serbia, and Montenegro should be evacuated....

12. The Turkish portions of the present Ottoman Empire should be assured a secure sovereignty, but the other nationalities which are now under Turkish rule should be assured an undoubted security of life and... unmolested opportunity of autonomous development....

13. An independent Polish state should be erected....

14. A general association of nations [League of Nations] must be formed under specific covenants for...affording mutual guarantees of political independence and territorial integrity to great and small states alike.

Source: Albert Shaw, ed., President Wilson's State Papers and Addresses. New York: The Review of Reviews Company, 1918, pp. 468-70. Originally published in 1917.

Wilson proposed a central body called The League of Nations to settle international disputes. The League of Nations was formed in January of 1920, with its headquarters at Geneva, Switzerland. The 63 member nations included all the major European powers. However, to Wilson's great disappointment, the U.S. Senate kept America out of the league.

Further, some decisions made in the peace settlement at Versailles, France, would create conflict in the future. Many historians believe that the harsh penalties placed on Germany made that country unstable, and actually helped Adolph Hitler come to power. Just 20 years later, the world would fight another great war with even more terrible weapons.

Research Activities/Things to Do

For soldiers in World War 1, as in other wars, songs provided diversion and expression of common sentiments. The song lyrics included here record a soldier's response, both to the new horrors of modern warfare and to the more general disillusion of men in combat.

- "Bombed Last Night" uses gallows humor to tame the dread of poison gas.... Evaluate the song.

Source: "Bombed Last Night": Singing at the Front in World War I. Found on http://history matters.gmu.edu

Bombed Last Night

Bombed last night, Bombed the night before

Gonna get bombed tonight if we never get bombed any more.
When we're bombed, we're scared as we can be.
Oh God damn the bombin'planes from Germany.

They're over us, they're over us,
One shell-hole for the four of us
Glory be to God there are no more of us
'Cause one of us could fill it all alone.

Gassed last night-gassed the night before,
Gonna get gassed again if we never git gassed no more,
When we're gassed, we're as sick as we can be,
'Cause phosgene and mustard gas is too much for me.

. . . .

Analyze this poster

1. What is the subject of this poster?

2. Who is the audience for the poster?

3. Is the poster trying to sell a product, an idea, or a call to action? Explain.

4. What is the message of the poster, in your own words:

5. Are the pictures symbolic of something? If so, what?

6. If the poster is historic, can you guess when it was posted?

Source: Found at www.swansongrp.com/picdocs/wwitoon.html

- The simple cartoon above was found attached to a letter from an American Soldier in WWI on the front in France. How does this convey the importance from hearing from loved ones at home?

- American Indians were drafted in huge numbers to fight in WWI. Like Blacks, they served in segregated units. But unlike Blacks, they were not American citizens with voting rights, so many opposed their forced military duty. Most American Indians did not become U.S. citizens until the American Indian Citizenship Act of 1924. If they refused the draft, they were sent to jail. Following is an excerpt from Carlos Montezuma, from a letter he wrote to Simon Kahanados, a Native American from Wisconsin. Do you agree with his position? Explain your answer.

Source: Montezuma Moore and The Papers of Joseph W. Lattmer. (Microfilm) Roll 4. Wilmington, Delaware: Scholarly Resources Inc., n.d., C.R.H.E.U. Found at http://raven.cc.ukans.edu/_kansite/ww_one/comment/Cmrts/Cmrt5.html#11

I do not think it is just for the Superintendents of the Indian service to get Indian young men to go to war. Why, because the United States Government has not given freedom to these young men. The Indian young men would be fighting for the United States government that is keeping them as slaves and not citizens of their own country. It does not look right to me or to those who love justice. The Indian is competent to be a soldier but not a citizen. That does not look right either. [The] Indian that does not vote and lives from the Government he cannot (be) drafted or forced into the war.

Suggested Further Reading

The books listed below are suggested readings in American literature, which tie in with the *Researching American History Series*. The selections were made based on feedback from teachers and librarians currently using them in interdisciplinary classes for students in grades 5 to 12. Of course there are many other historical novels that would be appropriate to tie in with the titles in this series.

After the Dancing Days, Margaret Rostkowski - M

Goodbye, Billy Radish, Gloria Skurzynski - M

War Horse, Michael Morpurgo - M

Starting from Home - A memoir, Milton Meltzer - M

Singing Tree, Kate Seredy - M

War Game, Michael Foreman - EL/M

A Farewell to Arms, Ernest Hemingway -HS

All Quiet on the Western Front, Erich Maria Remarque - HS

Johnny Got His Gun, T. Trumbo - HS

World War I: The Great War, A.J. Scopino, Jr., ed., nonfiction